WITH JESUS
I am Smart

This book belongs to:

....

....

Copyrights

WITH JESUS

I am Smart

Coloring Book Edition

Good News Meditations Kids

To receive print-ready samples from the coloring book version of this book, please go to gnmkids.com/free

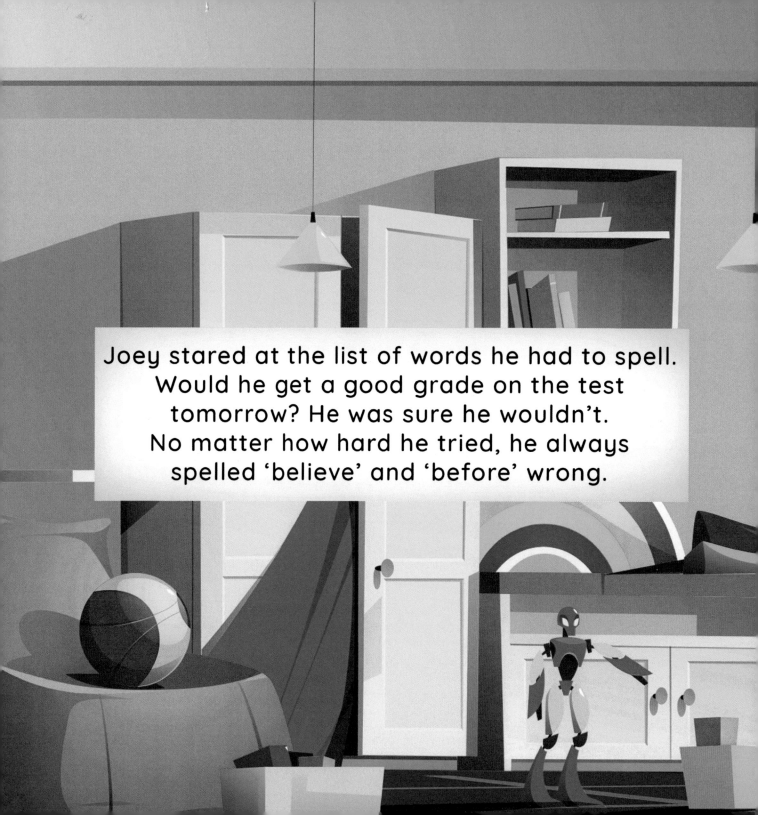

Joey stared at the list of words he had to spell. Would he get a good grade on the test tomorrow? He was sure he wouldn't. No matter how hard he tried, he always spelled 'believe' and 'before' wrong.

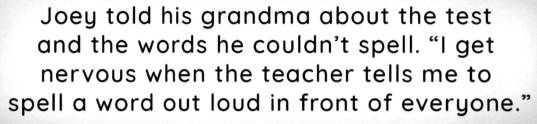

Joey told his grandma about the test and the words he couldn't spell. "I get nervous when the teacher tells me to spell a word out loud in front of everyone."

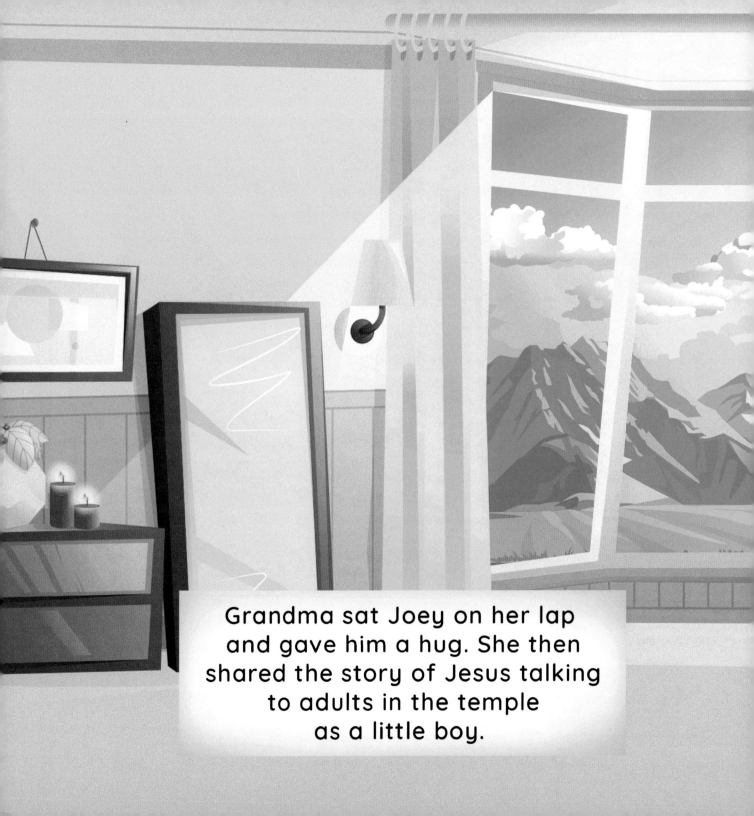

Grandma sat Joey on her lap and gave him a hug. She then shared the story of Jesus talking to adults in the temple as a little boy.

"Even though Jesus was a child, he wasn't scared to answer the questions adults asked Him because He knew that God was with Him. And that made Him smart. And now, Jesus lives in you."

Joey felt much better after talking to Grandma.

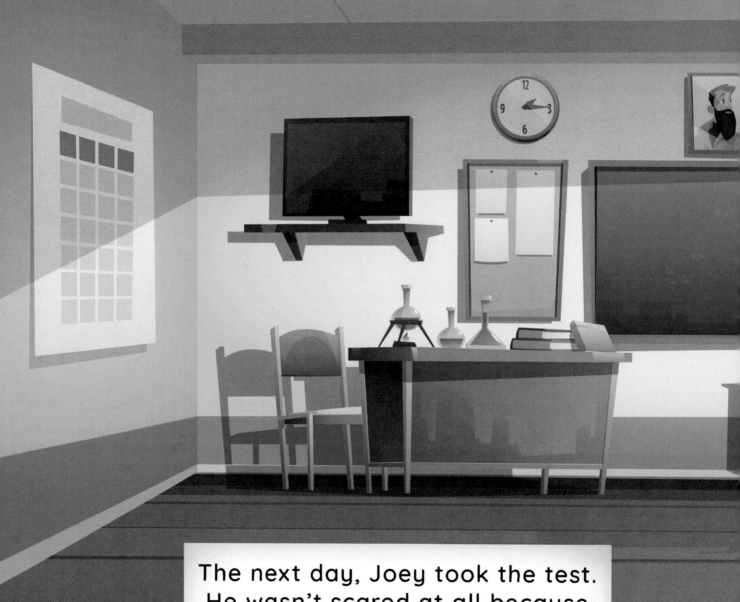

The next day, Joey took the test. He wasn't scared at all because he knew Jesus was with him.

After school, he hurried home to Grandma.

"I'm proud of you, Joey," Grandma said with a smile. "And so is Jesus."

The End.

And it came to pass, that after three days they found him in the temple, sitting in the midst of the doctors, both hearing them, and asking them questions. And all that heard him were astonished at his understanding and answers.

Luke 2:46-47 KJV

Author's note:

Thank you so much for reading this book. If you enjoyed this book, we would love it if you could leave a review and recommend it to a friend.

If there is anything you would like to share with us to help us improve this book, please go to gnmkids.com/feedback

Please checkout our other books

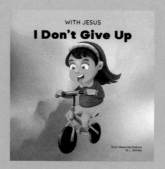

www.gnmkids.com